My First Bilingual

A B C

🇫🇷 Français - English 🇺🇸

Written by Cindy Cauley
Illustrated by Eléonore Clergeau

ISBN 979-8-9865268-0-5

First US Edition 2022.
Published by Cindy Cauley

THIS BOOK BELONGS TO :

....

A

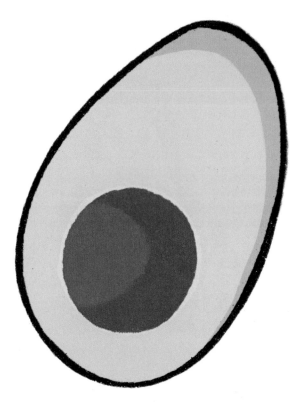

AVOCAT

AVOCADO

B

BIBERON

BOTTLE

C

CHAT
CAT

D

DOCTEUR
DOCTOR

E

ENVELOPPE

ENVELOPE

F

FOURCHETTE
FORK

G

GORILLE

GORILLA

H

HÉRISSON

HEDGEHOG

I

IGLOU
IGLOO

J

JUS

JUICE

K

KETCHUP

KETCHUP

L

LION

LION

M

MONTAGNE

MOUNTAIN

N

NID

NEST

O

ORANGE

ORANGE

P

PALMIER

PALM TREE

Q

QUICHE

QUICHE

R

RADIS

RADISH

S

SERPENT

SNAKE

T

TRAIN

TRAIN

U

UKULÉLÉ

UKULELE

V

VOLCAN
VOLCANO

W

WAGON

WAGON

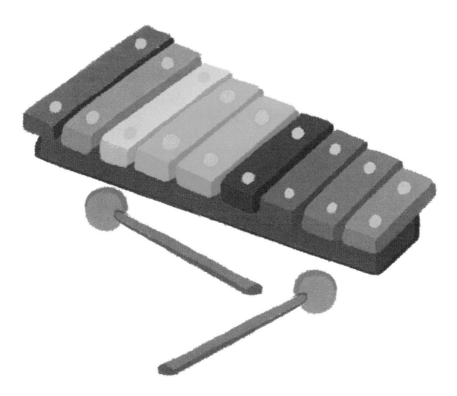

XYLOPHONE
XYLOPHONE

Y

YÉTI

YETI

Z

ZÈBRE

ZEBRA

FIN

THE
END

Behind the book

The Illustrator

Éléonore is a French illustrator based in Troyes, France. She has been passionate about drawing as long as she can remember and she started to work as an illustrator in 2020. She focuses on delivering art for children and hopes it will impact little ones and their parents. Find her on Instagram @byleodrawings

The Writer

Cindy is a Franco-American writer living in the USA since 2013. She has two young bilingual kids and is inspired to help multicultural families with their unique experiences. She created the podcast "Expat Families" and developed an online hub for children called "My Creative".

Made in the USA
Columbia, SC
31 March 2023

14601824R00020